■ Cross Stitcher ■

Magazine's book of

Country Animals

IN CROSS STITCH

Cross Stitcher

Magazine's book of

Country Animals

IN CROSS STITCH

Debra Page

future
BOOKS

Dedication

To my family

First published in 1995 by
Future Books
A division of Future Publishing Limited
30 Monmouth Street, Bath BA1 2BW

Designed by Maria Bowers
Illustrations by Kate Davies
Text by Amanda Clarkson
Photographic styling by Paula Mabe
Photography by Jonathan Fisher

A catalogue record of this book is available from the British Library

ISBN: 1 85981 085 3

Printed and bound in Malaysia by Times Offset (M) Sdn. Bhd.

We take great care to ensure that what we print is accurate, but we cannot accept liability for any mistakes or misprints.

CONTENTS

TECHNIQUES

HOW TO PREPARE THE FABRIC

To calculate the amount of fabric you need, add 2in (5cm) all the way round the finished stitched design area, or if it is going to be a framed picture then add 4in (10cm). Make sure that you cut the edges of the fabric straight by following the holes. The fabric should not fray as you stitch or the ends may catch in the stitching. You will also lose the neat edge which will make it difficult to make up or frame the finished piece. There are several ways of ensuring your fabric doesn't fray. A quick and simple method is to fold masking tape around the edges of the fabric. Another method is to stitch the raw edges either by working blanket stitch or overcasting round the edges or by machine with a zigzag stitch. For large pieces of fabric it is best to hem the edges by hand or machine.

HOW TO WORK FROM THE CHARTS

Each symbol on the chart represents one stitch and its position is counted on the fabric using the chart as a guide. Parts of the design may be outlined in back stitch; this is identified by the solid and dotted heavy lines around or through the symbols. The key tells you which symbols represent which colours on the chart and how many strands of thread to use. The pieces are stitched in the threads that are listed in the first column of the key. As the different manufacturer's threads are not exact equivalents, it is advisable to check the colours by eye before you begin stitching if you are going to use a different brand of thread. Other stitches, such as French knots, are listed at the end of the key. We also give details of the finished size that your project will be, so in each case you will have all you need to know.

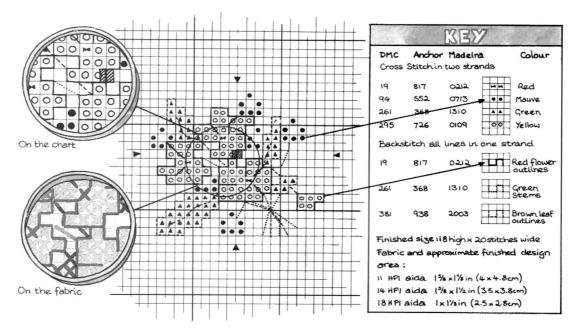

On the chart

On the fabric

KEY

DMC	Anchor	Madeira		Colour
Cross Stitch in two strands				
19	817	0212		Red
94	552	0713		Mauve
261	368	1310		Green
295	726	0109		Yellow
Backstitch all lines in one strand				
19	817	0212		Red flower outlines
261	368	1310		Green stems
381	938	2003		Brown leaf outlines

Finished size : 18 high x 20 stitches wide
Fabric and approximate finished design area :
11 HPI aida 1⅝ x 1⅞ in (4 x 4.8cm)
14 HPI aida 1⅜ x 1½ in (3.5 x 3.8cm)
18 HPI aida 1 x 1½ in (2.5 x 2.8cm)

RATINGS

At the beginning of each project you will find two sets of icons. The alarm clocks indicate the approximate time it would take an average stitcher of the suggested skill level to complete the project.

 1 AN EVENING

  2 A WEEK

 3 LESS THAN A MONTH

 4 MORE THAN A MONTH

The skill ratings indicate the level of experience required to stitch the project.

 EASY

 INTERMEDIATE

 SKILLED

 **EXPERT**

HOW TO MOUNT FABRIC IN AN EMBROIDERY HOOP

You should use a frame that is suitable for the size of the piece of fabric you are stitching on. It is better to mount your fabric into a hoop or frame as they keep the tension of the stitches even and give the stitching a much neater finish. They also help prevent the fabric from distorting.

There are various different types of hoops and frames available including wooden, plastic and rotating frames. Hoops hold a section of the fabric taut between two rings, and frames keep the entire piece of fabric taut.

If you are using a hoop, place the inner ring of the hoop under the fabric directly below the area you wish to stitch. Loosen the screw on the outer ring and place this over the fabric and inner ring, pushing down over it (illus. 1).

Tighten the screw so that the outer ring fits

over the inner ring and fabric, then gently pull the edges of the fabric beyond the hoop so that it is tight. It should be 'drum-tight' when you tap it (illus. 2).

If you want to protect your fabric from the hoop, which is especially important with fine fabrics, wrap fabric tape around the inner ring. Make sure that it overlaps as you wrap it round so that all the ring is covered then fasten it at the end by stitching into place.

When using a rotating frame, stitch the edges of the fabric to the end bars then attach the side arms. For a stretcher frame make sure the fabric is positioned centrally over the frame then staple the fabric round the stretcher bars and onto the back, making sure that the fabric is taut.

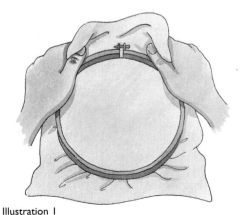

Illustration 1

Illustration 2

HOW TO SIZE YOUR DESIGN

I have given approximate finished design sizes for all the projects but you may want to calculate how big a design will be on a different count fabric. Simply divide the number of stitches on the chart by the number of holes per inch (HPI) of your fabric.

For example, the bluebell design shown is 11 stitches high and 10 stitches wide. If you are stitching on 14 HPI aida you need to calculate the height :

$11 \div 14 = \frac{7}{8}$ in (22mm) and the width $10 \div 14 = \frac{3}{4}$ in (19mm).

However, if you are stitching over two threads of the fabric you must divide the HPI by two before calculating the finished design area.

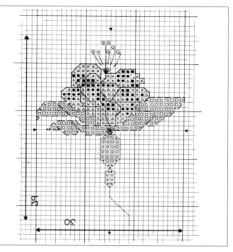

HOW TO WORK CROSS STITCH

Make a full cross stitch for each symbol on the chart. Bring the needle up at 1, down at 2, up at 3 and down at 4.

If you are working a block of stitches of the same colour, first work all the half stitches in one direction. Turn and work back along the row completing all the crosses.

HOW TO STITCH OVER TWO THREADS

If you are working on a high count fabric such as 28 HPI evenweave or linen, it is usual to stitch over two threads of the fabric. This will give the same finished design area as 14 HPI aida. Likewise, if you are working on 36 HPI linen you will get the same area as 18 HPI aida. Make each stitch cross over two threads to cover a nine hole square instead of the usual four hole square.

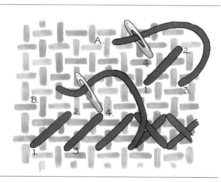

HOW TO STITCH BACK STITCH

Follow the solid or dotted lines for the back stitch using the number of strands which are indicated in the key.

Make the first stitch from left to right. Pass the needle behind the fabric, and bring it out one stitch length ahead to the left. Repeat and continue along the line in this way.

HOW TO STITCH FRENCH KNOTS

Bring the needle up where you want the knot to be. Hold the thread where it comes out of the fabric with your left hand. For a small knot, twist the needle round the thread once; for a large knot, twist it round two or three times. Holding the thread taut, push the needle down into the fabric close to where it emerged.

When the needle is halfway through the fabric, tighten the thread close up to the needle to form a knot. Continue pushing the needle and thread back to the wrong side of the fabric.

HOW TO STITCH THREE-QUARTER AND QUARTER STITCH

If there is a symbol in the corner of a square, you should make a three-quarter stitch in that position. The symbol will be a smaller version of the full stitch symbol shown in the key. First, work a quarter stitch by bringing the needle up at that corner and pushing it down in the centre then stitch the diagonal half stitch across it. If you are working over one thread such as with 14 HPI aida then you will have to split the threads in the centre.

Where two different symbols share a square on the chart, one is a three-quarter stitch in one colour and one is a quarter stitch in another colour. It is up to you which colour you choose to be the main colour, but it is better if the three-quarter stitch is in the colour you want to be more prominent.

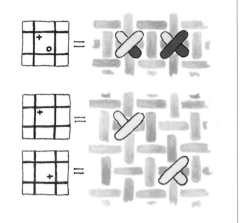

FRENCH KNOTS (continued)

If you are left-handed, hold the needle in your left hand and the thread in your right. Twist the needle clockwise round the thread. Keeping the thread in your right hand, insert the needle into the fabric to the left of the original hole where the thread emerged and pull up the thread in order to tighten the knot. Push the needle through the fabric.

HOW TO WASH YOUR FINISHED STITCHING

If you notice any marks on your finished work, you can wash it. Immerse the stitched piece in luke-warm water. If the colours start to run, don't worry, just keep rinsing until the water runs clear. If there are any stubborn stains, rub a little detergent on to the area until the stain is removed.

● Roll the wet fabric in a towel to remove excess water.

● Pad your ironing board with a thick, clean, white towel. Place your work right side down on this with a thin clean cloth over it. Press carefully until the fabric is dry. The thickness of the towel will prevent you from flattening the stitches.

Iron into the stitches with the point of the iron in a circular motion - this will raise the stitches and improve their appearance. Be careful to avoid having the iron too hot or pressing too hard.

HOW TO MOUNT YOUR WORK IN A SMALL FRAME

Should you wish to mount your work in a small frame, hold the frame in both hands, pushing out the clear plastic and snap-in plastic back, with your thumbs.

Place the clear plastic centrally over your stitched fabric and draw round it with a pencil. Cut a piece of light-weight iron-on interfacing slightly larger than the clear plastic then iron it on the back of the stitching.

Cut round the pencil line. If you want to pad

HOW TO MOUNT YOUR WORK IN A SMALL FRAME (continued)

your work and not place the clear plastic front inside then cut a piece of 2 oz. wadding the same size as the fabric.

Place the stitched fabric then the wadding into the frame. Finally push the plastic back behind them into the frame. If you want to use the clear plastic front put this in first then the stitching and finally the plastic back to complete.

HOW TO LACE YOUR WORK FOR FRAMING

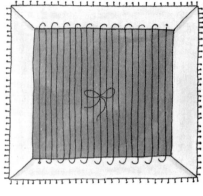

Illustration 1

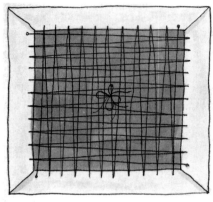

Illustration 2

Cut a piece of acid free mount board to the same size as the inside of the frame. This will be your lacing board.

If you want to use a coloured mount inside your frame then cut a piece of 2oz. wadding to the same size as the mount opening. If you are not using a mount then cut the wadding to the size of the frame opening. Place the wadding centrally on the lacing board.

Centre your stitched fabric right side up over the wadding and lacing board. Push pins through the fabric and into the board along the top edge. Use the holes of the fabric as a guide to ensure that you pin it straight.

Pull the fabric gently and pin along the bottom in the same way. Repeat this for the other two sides.

Working from the back of the board, thread a large-eyed needle with thick strong cotton such as crochet cotton and tie a knot at the end. Lace from top to bottom using an under and over motion. Stop halfway across the back and repeat the lacing for the other side. When you reach the centre, go back and remove the slack from the threads by pulling them tightly one by one. Once you have done this, knot the two ends at the centre (illus. 1).

Repeat this process from side to side. If at any stage you run out of thread before you reach the centre, join a new piece with a reef knot.

Fold in the corners and stitch into place then remove the pins. Your work is now ready to be framed (illus. 2).

HOW TO MOUNT YOUR STITCHING INTO A CARD

Place strips of double sided tape on the inside of B at the edges of the card.

Place your finished design face upwards on the table. Turn your card over and hold it centrally above the stitched design. Press the card down on the table until it holds firmly.

Turn the card over so that it is face down with the base of the design towards you. Place strips of double sided tape on the outside edges of A. Place the wadding over the back of the stitched fabric and press down A onto B, making sure that the wadding stays in place as you do this.

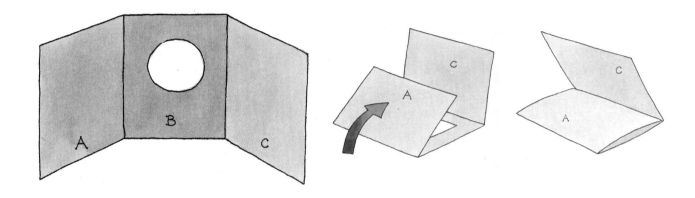

HOW TO MAKE YOUR DESIGN INTO A CUSHION

MAKING YOUR STITCHED PIECE INTO A CUSHION

1 Trim the finished design to a10x10in (25.4x25.4cm) square.

2 Pin one velvet strip right sides together with an edge of the aida. Make sure its placed centrally so that 4in (10.2cm) of the strip are either side of the aida. (illus. 1).

3 Sew the fabric and the aida together with a 1in (2.5cm) allowance. You will find it easier to achieve a straight line if the aida is uppermost; you can follow the holes in the aida. Do not sew right to the edges of the aida; leave an inch either side. (illus. 1).

4 Repeat this process for the three other sides. Be careful not to sew into the strips already attached.

5 With the design right side down, iron the seams flat, but upwards. Do not open out the seams and press. You are now ready to mitre the corners.

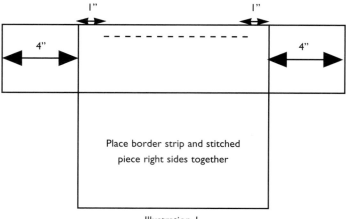

Place border strip and stitched piece right sides together

Illustration 1

HOW TO MITRE THE CORNERS

1 Lay the aida, with border strips attached, right side down. Concentrating on one corner at a time, fold one border strip over the other and pin. Using tailors chalk or a white pencil and a ruler, draw a straight line at an angle of 45° from the inner corner on to the fabric (illus 2.).

2 Swap over the positions of the two border strips and repeat this step. You will now have a stitching line marked on both pieces of the border (illus. 3).

3 With right sides together, match up the pencil lines and pin them together. Sew the two border pieces together along the line. Make sure you start sewing at exactly the point where the seams meet. Press the seam open (illus. 4).

4 Now mitre the other three corners in the same way.

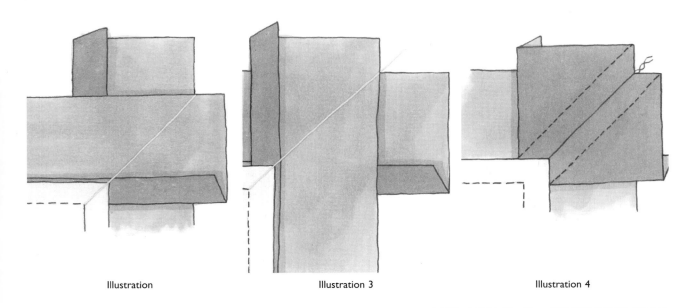

Illustration   Illustration 3   Illustration 4

HOW TO FINISH

1 Place the cushion cover front and back right sides together. Pin all the way round the edge.

2 Stitch round the edge with a 1in (2.5cm) seam allowance, leaving an opening on one side big enough to insert the cushion pad.

3 Turn the cover right sides out and insert the cushion pad. Sew up the opening with tiny invisible stitches.

13

HEDGEHOG

This simple design makes up into
a charming greetings card
suitable for any occasion.

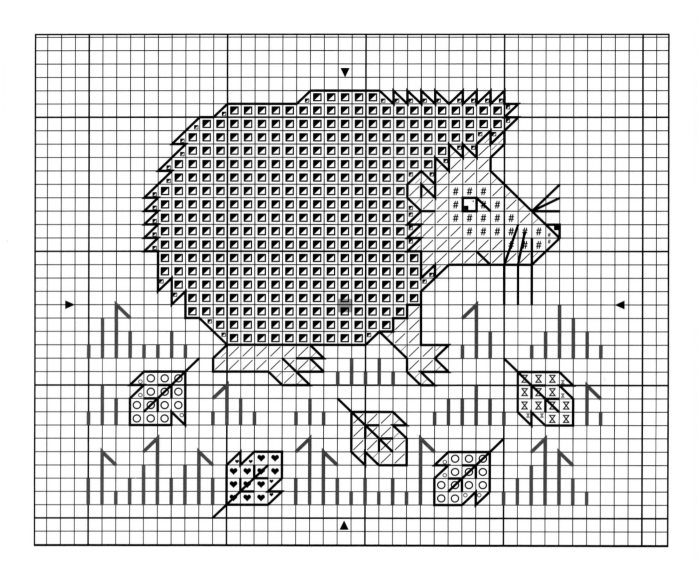

HOW TO STITCH

It is best to start stitching from the centre – this ensures an even amount of fabric all round the design. Find the centre of your fabric by folding it lightly in half both ways. The centre of the chart is indicated by a grey square.

Work the cross stitch first using two strands of stranded cotton. The spines of the hedgehog are stitched by blending one strand of one colour with one strand of another colour. Refer to the key for colour details.

When you have completed the cross stitch, you can work the backstitch.
Use one strand of very dark brown for all the hedgehog's outlines and details and for the leaves. Use two strands of green for the grass.

Once all the stitching is complete, you are ready to mount your design in the card.

YOU WILL NEED

- 18HPI aida - 4½x3½in (11.4x8.9cm), cream
- Stranded cotton - as listed in the key
- Tapestry needle - size 24
- Card - with a 2½x2½in (6.4x6.4cm) opening, cream
- Double-sided tape

As the only spiny mammal in Britain, the hedgehog commands a popular following. Although it hibernates for half the year, the hedgehog creates a stir when it's awake, by nesting in bonfires!

HEDGEHOG KEY

ANCHOR	DMC	MADEIRA		COLOUR
Cross stitch in two strands				
002	White	White	· ·	White
065	915	0704	♥ ♥	Cerise
297	726	0105	o o	Yellow
304	741	0201	x x	Orange
403	310	Black	■ ■	Black
888	371	2108	# #	Medium brown
943	422	2012	/ /	Light brown
Cross stitch blending one strand of each				
906	829	2113		Dark brown
942	739	2014		Very light brown
Backstitch all lines in one strand				
381	938	2003		Very dark brown outlines & details of hedgehog & leaves
Backstitch all lines in two strands				
210	562	1312		Green grass stalks

Our model was stitched using Anchor threads; the DMC and Madeira conversions are not necessarily exact colour equivalents.
Finished size: Stitch count 32 high x 37 wide
Fabric and approximate finished design area:
11HPI aida 2⅞x3⅜in   **14HPI** aida 2¼x2⅝in
18HPI aida 1¾x2in

HOW TO MOUNT YOUR STITCHING IN THE CARD

See illus. page 11. Place strips of double-sided tape on the inside of B at the edges and around the opening. Place your finished design face upwards on the table. Turn the card over and hold it with the opening centred above the stitched design. Press card down onto design.

Turn the card over so that the design is face down and right way up. Place strips of double-sided tape close to the edges of A. Press A onto B firmly. Instead of double-sided tape, you can use glue, but avoid using too much and wipe away any excess immediately.

OTTER

Sewn onto a tackle bag, this design is guaranteed to inspire any angler who wishes to emulate the fishing skills of the otter!

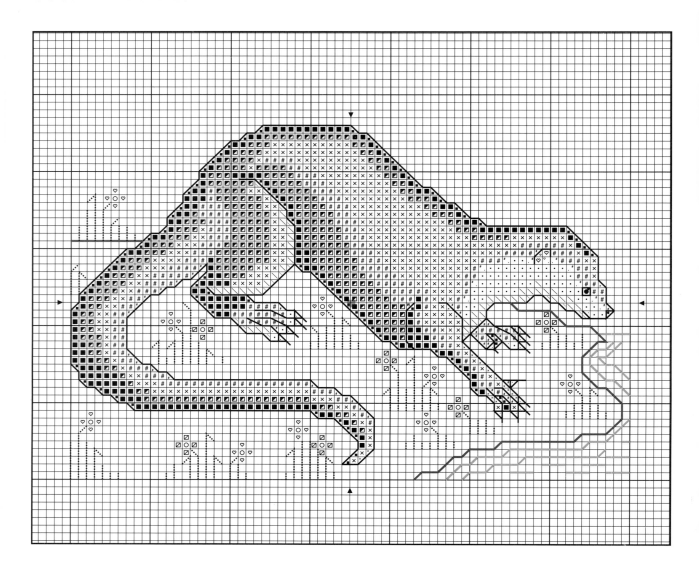

HOW TO STITCH

It is best to start stitching from the centre – this ensures an even amount of fabric all round the design. Find the centre of your fabric by folding it lightly in half both ways. The centre of the chart is indicated by a grey square.

Work the cross stitch first using two strands of stranded cotton.

When you have completed the cross stitch, you can work the following backstitch in one strand: very dark brown for the otter's

outlines and details; green for the grass and flower stems; blue for the water. Use two strands of green for the grass edges.

Finally work a French knot in one strand of white for the eye.

Once all the stitching is complete, trim the stitched design to within four squares of the stitched design. Turn under two squares all round and stitch to the flap of your rucksack with small neat stitches in a contrasting thread.

YOU WILL NEED

- 14HPI aida - 8x10in (20.3x25.4cm), cream
- Stranded cotton - as listed in the key
- Tapestry needle - size 24
- Rucksack
- Usual sewing kit - matching thread, needle etc.

Due to dwindling numbers, otters are legally protected, but in spite of their scarcity in lowland Britain, they are known to thrive on the west coast of Scotland. Sliding down ice banks into the water is a great source of family entertainment for otters!

OTTER KEY

ANCHOR	DMC	MADEIRA		COLOUR
Cross stitch in two strands				
008	353	0304	♡♡	Pink
291	444	0106	○○	Yellow
349	301	2306	××	Very light brown
352	400	2305	##	Light brown
358	801	2304	◪◪	Medium brown
380	938	2007	■■	Dark brown
386	746	2101	··	Light cream
390	822	1907	╲╲	Dark cream
403	310	Black	●●	Black
1016	3727	1711	⊘⊘	Mauve

ANCHOR	DMC	MADEIRA		COLOUR
Backstitch all lines in one strand				
169	517	1108		Blue water
228	700	1304		Green grass & flower stems
382	3371	2004		Very dark brown otter outlines

ANCHOR	DMC	MADEIRA		COLOUR
Backstitch all lines in two strands				
228	700	1304		Green grass edges

ANCHOR	DMC	MADEIRA		COLOUR
Stitch french knots in one strand				
001	White	White	··	White eye highlight

Our model was stitched using Anchor threads; the DMC and Madeira conversions are not necessarily exact colour equivalents.

Finished size: Stitch count 46 high x 70 wide
Fabric and approximate finished design area:
11HPI aida 4⅛x6⅜in   14HPI aida 3¼x5in
18HPI aida 2½x3⅞in

FOX

A beautiful study of nature, this design makes up into a superb framed picture.

HOW TO STITCH

Be sure to stitch this design in good light as the subtle shading of the fox's fur can make this a little tricky, particularly when counting your place.

It is best to start stitching from the centre – this ensures an even amount of fabric all round the design. Find the centre of your fabric by folding it lightly in half both ways. The centre of the chart is indicated by a grey square.

Work the cross stitch first using two strands of stranded cotton. Some areas on the fox's coat and legs are stitched by blending one strand of one colour with one strand of another. Refer to the key for colour details.

When you have completed the cross stitch, you can work the backstitch.
Use one strand of very dark brown for all the fox's outlines and details. Use two strands of green for the ferns.

YOU WILL NEED

- 14HPI aida - 13x12in (33x30.5cm), cream
- Stranded cotton - as listed in the key
- Tapestry needle - size 24
- Frame - 9x8¾in (22.9x22.2cm), gilt finish
- Mount - with a 5½x5¼in (14x13.3cm) opening, green
- 2oz wadding - 5½x5¼in (14x13.3cm)

The fox has gradually discovered and exploited the rich pickings of urban environments, and it is not unheard of to see them in Trafalgar Square in London!

Finally, create the whites of the eyes with a French knot in each, worked in one strand of white stranded cotton.

Once all the stitching is complete, you can wash and prepare your work for framing following the instructions in the techniques pages at the beginning of the book.

FOX KEY

ANCHOR	DMC	MADEIRA		COLOUR
Cross stitch in two strands				
001	White	White	· ·	White
314	741	0201	o o	Orange
363	436	2011	J J	Light brown
380	839	1913	✗ ✗	Dark brown
400	317	1714	● ●	Grey
403	310	Black	■ ■	Black
830	644	1814		Cream
Cross stitch blending one strand of each				
363	436	2011	X X	Light brown
365	434	2009		Medium brown
365	434	2009	◄ ◄	Medium brown
380	839	1913		Dark brown
380	839	1913	◢ ◢	Dark brown
403	310	Black		Black
400	317	1714	x x	Grey
830	644	1814		Cream
Backstitch all lines in one strand				
382	3371	2004		Very dark brown fox outlines & details
Backstitch all lines in two strands				
238	703	1307		Green ferns
Stitch French knots in one strand				
001	White	White	· ·	White eye highlights

Our model was stitched using Anchor threads; the DMC and Madeira conversions are not necessarily exact colour equivalents.

Finished size: Stitch count 60 high x 56 wide
Fabric and approximate finished design area:
11HPI aida 5⅜x5in   14HPI aida 4¼x4in
18HPI aida 3⅜x3⅛in

MOLE

Gardener's friend or gardener's enemy? Either way, this cheerful design makes the perfect adornment to any gardening accessory.

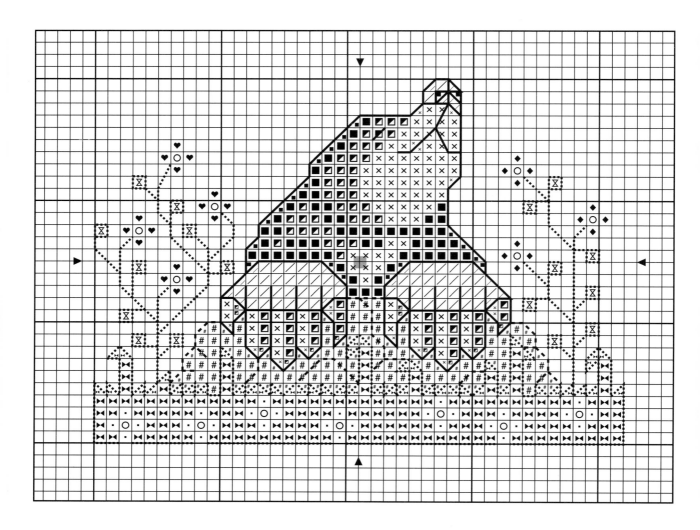

HOW TO STITCH

Brighten up a plain sun hat with this cute mole design. You might also like to stitch it for an item of clothing.

It is best to start stitching from the centre – this ensures an even amount of fabric all round the design. Find the centre of your fabric by folding it lightly in half both ways. The centre of the chart is indicated by a grey square.

Work the cross stitch first using two strands of stranded cotton.

When you have completed the cross stitch, you can work the following backstitch in one strand: black for the mole's outlines and details; dark brown for the molehill; dark green for the flower stems and to outline the grass and leaves.

Once all the stitching is complete, trim the fabric four squares all round the design. Turn under two squares to make a neat edge and sew to the front of the hat with tiny invisible stitches.

28

YOU WILL NEED

- 14HPI aida - 5x6in (12.7x15.2cm), white
- Stranded cotton - as listed in the key
- Tapestry needle - size 24
- Sun hat - cotton, blue
- Usual sewing kit - matching thread, needle, etc.

In a letter to Kenneth Grahame on the subject of *The Wind in the Willows* in 1909, President Roosevelt expressed his delight in the book, referring to Mole and his companions as 'old friends'.

MOLE KEY

ANCHOR	DMC	MADEIRA		COLOUR
Cross stitch in two strands			
001	White	White	· ·	White
008	353	0304	/ /	Light pink
054	956	0611	♥ ♥	Dark pink
228	700	1304	⋈ ⋈	Medium green
235	317	1801	× ×	Light grey
256	906	1401	Σ Σ	Light green
291	444	0106	○ ○	Yellow
355	975	2008	# #	Light brown
400	413	1714	◨	Dark grey
403	310	Black	■ ■	Black
433	996	1103	◆ ◆	Blue

ANCHOR	DMC	MADEIRA		COLOUR
Backstitch all lines in one strand			
381	938	2003		Dark brown outlines & details of mound
403	310	Black		Black outlines & details of mole
879	890	1705		Dark green grass, flower stems & leaves

Our model was stitched using Anchor threads; the DMC and Madeira conversions are not necessarily exact colour equivalents.

Finished size: Stitch count 30 high x 42 wide
Fabric and approximate finished design area:
11HPI aida 2¾x3⅞in   14HPI aida 2⅛x3in
18HPI aida 1⅝x2⅜in

RABBIT

Everybody's favourite country animal, here stylishly presented in a design which will delight both children and adults alike.

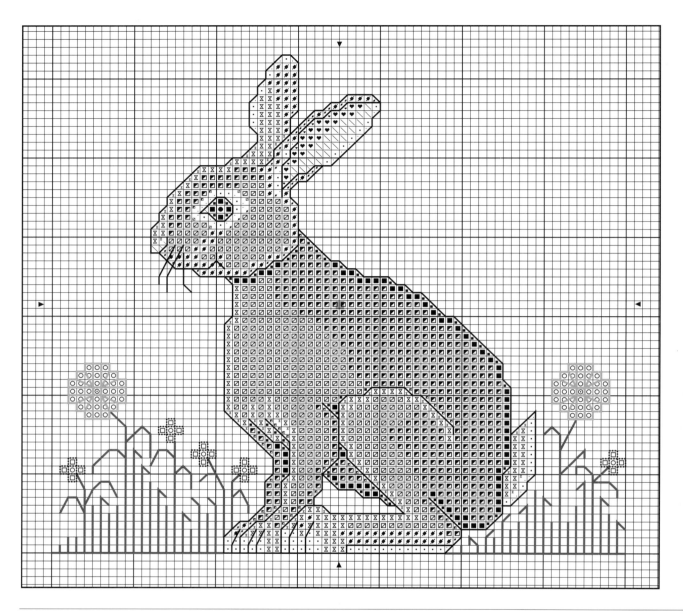

HOW TO STITCH

It is best to start stitching from the centre – this ensures an even amount of fabric all round the design. Find the centre of your fabric by folding it lightly in half both ways. The centre of the chart is indicated by a grey square.

Work the cross stitch first using two strands of stranded cotton. The shading on the rabbit's fur is created by blending one strand of one colour with one strand of another colour. Refer to the key for colour details. Careful

counting is required, especially round by the rabbit's forelegs where there is a lot of colour change.

When you have completed the cross stitch, you can work the following backstitch in one strand: dark brown for the rabbit's outlines and details; dark pink to outline the yellow flowers; dark blue for the flower outlines. Use two strands of green for both the grass and the flower stems.

YOU WILL NEED

- 14HPI aida - 12x12in (30.5x30.5cm), white
- Stranded cotton - as listed in the key
- Tapestry needle - size 24
- Frame - 9¼x9½in (23.5x24.1cm), dark wood with gilt trim
- Mount - with a 5½x5¾in (14x14.6cm) opening, beige
- 2oz wadding - 5½x5¾in (14x14.6cm)

The popularity of the furry, lop-eared, happy-go-lucky rabbit has resulted in some legendary characters, among them, Bugs Bunny, Peter Rabbit and Roger Rabbit.

Finally, create the white of the eye with a French knot worked in white stranded cotton.

Once all the stitching is complete, you can wash and prepare your work for framing following the instructions in the techniques pages at the beginning of the book.

RABBIT KEY

ANCHOR	DMC	MADEIRA		COLOUR
Cross stitch in two strands				
002	White	White		White
131	798	0911		Light blue
297	726	0105		Yellow
316	740	0203		Orange
358	433	2008		Medium brown
360	898	2006		Dark brown
373	422	2103		Light brown
403	310	Black		Black
881	950	2309		Light pink
883	3064	2312		Dark pink
Cross stitch blending one strand of each				
358	433	2008		Medium brown
390	822	1908		Beige
373	422	2103		Light brown
390	822	1908		Beige
Backstitch all lines in one strand				
132	797	0912		Dark blue flower outlines
381	3371	2003		Very dark brown rabbit outlines & details
883	3064	2312		Dark pink dandelion outlines
Backstitch all lines in two strands				
230	910	1302		Green plant stems & grass stalks
Stitch French knots in two strands				
002	White	White		White eye highlight

Our model was stitched using Anchor threads; the DMC and Madeira conversions are not necessarily exact colour equivalents.

Finished size: Stitch count 63 high x 70 wide
Fabric and approximate finished design area:
11HPI aida 5¾x6⅜in   14HPI aida 4½x5in
18HPI aida 3½x3⅞in

DORMOUSE

Add a touch of individual style to your child's pencil case with this lovely sleepy dormouse design.

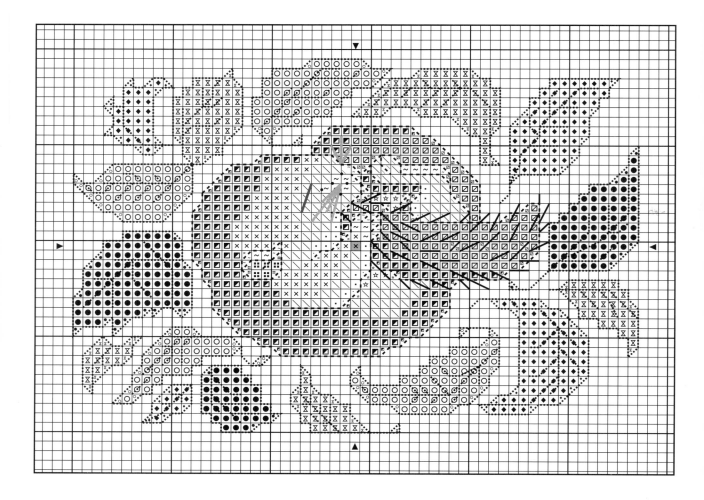

HOW TO STITCH

Careful counting is required for this design, especially when placing the leaves and the longstitch detail on the tail.

It is best to start stitching from the centre – this ensures an even amount of fabric all round the design. Find the centre of your fabric by folding it lightly in half both ways. The centre of the chart is indicated by a grey square.

Work the cross stitch first using two strands of stranded cotton. Areas on the mouse are stitched by blending one strand of one colour with one strand of another colour. Refer to the key for colour details.

When you have completed the cross stitch, you can work the following backstitch details

in one strand: grey for the mouse's outlines and details; very dark brown for the leaves, outlines and details. Stitch the zig-zag border with two strands of dark brown and the mouse's eye with two strands of black.

Work the mouse's whiskers using longstitch in one strand of beige.

Finally, work the French knots around its nose in one strand of black.

Once all the stitching is complete, trim the stitched design to within four squares of the border. Turn under two squares all round and stitch to the make-up bag with small neat stitches.

YOU WILL NEED

- **14HPI aida - 8x10in (20.3x25.4cm), white**
- **Stranded cotton - as listed in the key**
- **Tapestry needle - size 24**
- **Make-up bag**
- **Usual sewing kit - matching thread, needle, etc.**

At the turn of the century, with the demand for industrial output, the dormouse reaped the benefits of 'coppicing', the practice of growing small woods for producing charcoal. Coppices were ideal habitats for this now endangered mouse.

Our model was stitched using Anchor threads; the DMC and Madeira conversions are not necessarily exact colour equivalents.

Finished size: Stitch count 39 high x 57 wide
Fabric and approximate finished design area:
11HPI aida 3½x5⅛in
14HPI aida 2¾x4in
18HPI aida 2⅛x3⅛in

DORMOUSE KEY

ANCHOR	DMC	MADEIRA		COLOUR
Cross stitch in two strands				
275	746	0102		Cream
304	741	0203		Orange
308	782	2212		Light brown
355	400	2008		Medium brown
359	898	2006		Dark brown
868	758	2313		Light pink
883	3778	2312		Dark pink
Cross stitch blending one strand of each				
275	746	0102		Cream
295	727	0109		Light yellow
305	726	0107		Dark yellow
295	727	0109		Light yellow
305	726	0107		Dark yellow
400	414	1801		Grey
305	726	0107		Dark yellow
899	3782	2002		Beige
400	414	1801		Grey
275	746	0102		Cream
Backstitch all lines in one strand				
381	938	2003		Very dark brown outlines & details of leaves
400	414	1801		Grey outlines & details of dormouse
403	310	Black		Black tail details
Backstitch all lines in two strands				
403	310	Black		Black eye
Long stitch all lines in one strand				
899	3782	2002		Beige whiskers
Stitch French knots in one strand				
403	310	Black		Black whisker details

SQUIRREL

This foraging squirrel really comes to life in a design to keep you occupied through the long winter nights.

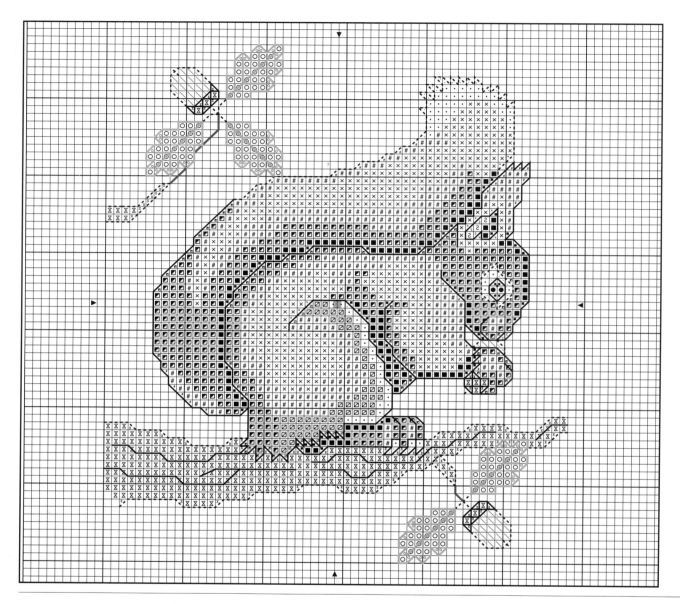

HOW TO STITCH

Be sure to stitch this design in good light as the subtle shading of the squirrel's coat and tail can make this a little tricky, particularly when counting your place.

It is best to start stitching from the centre – this ensures an even amount of fabric all round the design. Find the centre of your fabric by folding it lightly in half both ways. The centre of the chart is indicated by a grey square.

Work the cross stitch first using two strands

of stranded cotton. Some areas on the squirrel's coat and tail are stitched by blending one strand of one colour with one strand of another colour. Refer to the key for colour details.

When you have completed the cross stitch, you can work the following backstitch using one strand: black for the squirrel's body outlines and details and part of its tail, also for details on the branch and acorn cups; dark brown to outline the top part of tail, around

YOU WILL NEED

- 14HPI aida - 13x11in (33x27.9cm), white
- Stranded cotton - as listed in the key
- Tapestry needle - size 24
- Frame - 9x7in (22.9x17.8cm), oval, dark wood with gilt trim
- 2oz wadding - 6½x4½in (16.5x11.4cm) oval

The grey squirrel, keen to nibble from any garden bird table, has been known to outwit the most advanced obstacle courses with its nimble acrobatics, even to the extent of becoming a TV celebrity!

the eye area, the branches and acorns; green for the leaves, outlines and details. Use two strands of dark brown for the twig details.

Finally, create the white of the eye with a French knot worked in one strand of white stranded cotton.

Once all the stitching is complete, you can wash and prepare your work for framing following the instructions on the techniques pages at the beginning of the book.

SQUIRREL KEY

ANCHOR	DMC	MADEIRA		COLOUR
Cross stitch in two strands				
006	754	0305	s s	Pink
225	703	1307	o o	Light green
360	938	2005	■ ■	Dark brown
387	Ecru	Ecru	· ·	Ecru
403	310	Black	● ●	Black
856	730	1607	⊠ ⊠	Olive
887	3046	2208		Fawn
Cross stitch blending one strand of each				
349	301	2306	⊘ ⊘	Light terracotta
360	938	2005		Dark brown
351	400	2304	# #	Dark terracotta
349	301	2306		Light terracotta
351	400	2304	◪ ◪	Dark terracotta
360	938	2005		Dark brown
387	Ecru	Ecru	× ×	Ecru
349	301	2306		Light terracotta
Backstitch all lines in one strand				
218	699	1314		Dark green outlines & details of leaves
403	310	Black		Black squirrel & acorn cup outlines & details & details on branch
360	938	2005		Dark brown branch outlines
Backstitch all lines in two strands				
360	938	2005		Dark brown twig details
Stitch French knots in one strand				
001	White	White	· ·	White eye highlight

Our model was stitched using Anchor threads; the DMC and Madeira conversions are not necessarily exact colour equivalents.

Finished size: Stitch count 67 high x 58 wide

Fabric and approximate finished design area:

11HPI aida 6x5¼in   **14HPI** aida 4¾x4⅛in

18HPI aida 3¾x3¼in

BADGER

Brighten up the children's bedroom with an old woodland favourite who always inspires warmth and confidence.

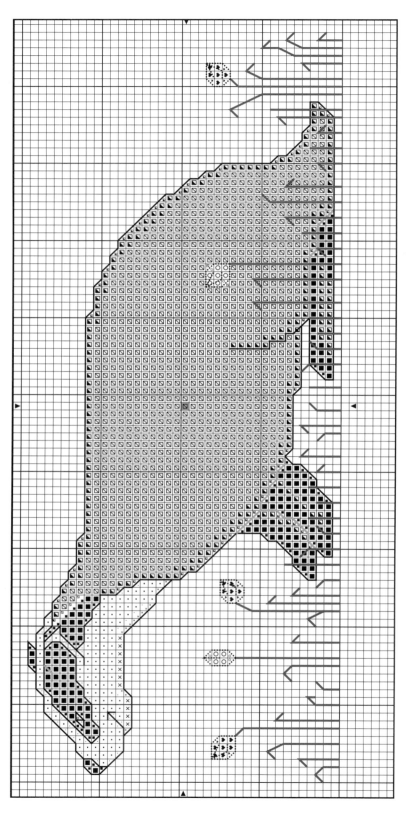

HOW TO STITCH

It is best to start stitching from the centre – this ensures an even amount of fabric all round the design. Find the centre of your fabric by folding it lightly in half both ways. The centre of the chart is indicated by a grey square.

Work the cross stitch first using two strands of stranded cotton. The badger's coat is stitched by blending one strand of one colour with one strand of another colour. Refer to the key for colour details. There is quite a large area to cover for the badger's body, so don't get carried away with stitching and forget to leave the squares free for the yellow flower. Count your stitches carefully.

When you have completed the cross stitch, you can work the following backstitch details in one strand: black for the badgers's outlines and details; light grey to separate the legs from the body and from each other; dark grey to outline the flowers. Use two strands of green for the grass and flower stems.

Once all the stitching is complete, you can wash and prepare your work for framing following the instructions on the techniques pages at the beginning of the book.

YOU WILL NEED

- 14HPI aida - 11x15in (27.9x38.1cm), white
- Stranded cotton - as listed in the key
- Tapestry needle - size 24
- Frame - 7½x11¾in (19x29.8cm), dark wood with gilt trim
- Mount - with a 3¾x8in (9.5x20.3cm) opening, red
- 2oz wadding - 3¾x8in (9.5x20.3cm)

A well-groomed Scots gentleman could thank a badger for his attire, as the hair from a badger was sought for making shaving bristles and to cover the sporran, worn over the kilt.

BADGER KEY

ANCHOR	DMC	MADEIRA		COLOUR
Cross stitch in two strands				
002	White	White		White
046	666	0210		Red
297	726	0105		Yellow
371	433	2008		Brown
397	762	1804		Light grey
403	310	Black		Black
Cross stitch blending in one strand of each				
400	317	1714		Dark grey
403	310	Black		Black
403	310	Black		Black
232	452	1807		Medium grey
Backstitch all lines in one strand				
397	762	1804		Light grey leg highlights
400	317	1714		Dark grey flower outlines
403	310	Black		Black badger outlines & details
Backstitch all lines in two strands				
228	700	1304		Green flower stems & grass stalks

Our model was stitched using Anchor threads; the DMC and Madeira conversions are not necessarily exact colour equivalents.

Finished size: Stitch count 39 high x 97 wide
Fabric and approximate finished design area:
11HPI aida 3½x8⅞in   **14HPI** aida 2¾x7in
18HPI aida 2⅛x5⅜in

STAG

The king of the countryside makes a noble adornment to a cushion, or would look equally good framed on the living room wall.

YOU WILL NEED

- **14HPI aida - 13x13in (33x33cm), white**
- **Stranded cotton - as listed in the key**
- **Tapestry needle - size 24**
- **Fabric - one 18x18in (45.7x45.7cm) square; four 5½x18in (14x45.7cm) strips; cotton, russet**
- **Uncovered cushion**
- **Usual sewing kit - matching thread, needle, etc.**

HOW TO STITCH

It is best to start stitching from the centre – this ensures an even amount of fabric all round the design. Find the centre of your fabric by folding it lightly in half both ways. The centre of the chart is indicated by a grey square.

Work the cross stitch first using two strands of stranded cotton. Some areas on the stag are stitched by blending one strand of one colour with one strand of another colour. Refer to the key for exact colour details.

When you have completed the cross stitch, you can work the following backstitch using one strand: dark brown to outline the stag; black for the outlines of the eyes, mouth and nose. Use two strands of green for the grass and flower stems.

Finally, create the white of the eye with a French knot worked in one strand of white stranded cotton.

STAG KEY

ANCHOR	DMC	MADEIRA		COLOUR
Cross stitch in two strands				
001	White	White	· ·	White
290	973	0105	○ ○	Yellow
313	977	2301	⊙ ⊙	Orange
349	301	2306	□ □	Light terracotta
352	300	2304	⋈ ⋈	Dark terracotta
358	433	2008	● ●	Light brown
360	898	2006	■ ■	Medium brown
387	822	Ecru		Light ecru
400	317	1714	# #	Grey
403	310	Black	◆ ◆	Black
830	644	1814	× ×	Dark ecru
Cross stitch blending one strand of each				
349	301	2306	⊠ ⊠	Light terracotta
830	644	1814		Dark ecru
349	301	2306	◪ ◪	Light terracotta
360	898	2006		Medium brown
Backstitch all lines in one strand				
382	3021	1810		Dark brown outlines of deer
403	310	Black		Black outlines of eyes, mouth & nose
Backstitch all lines in two strands				
255	907	1410		Green grass & flower stems
Stitch French knots in one strand				
001	White	White	· ·	White eye highlights

Our model was stitched using Anchor threads; the DMC and Madeira conversions are not necessarily exact colour equivalents.

Finished size: Stitch count 92 high x 88 wide
Fabric and approximate finished design area:
11HPI aida 8⅜x8in   **14HPI** aida 6½x6¼in
18HPI aida 5⅛x4⅞in

STOAT

This inquisitive little fellow adds a special touch to a walker's knap-sack or makes an ideal gift or greetings card!

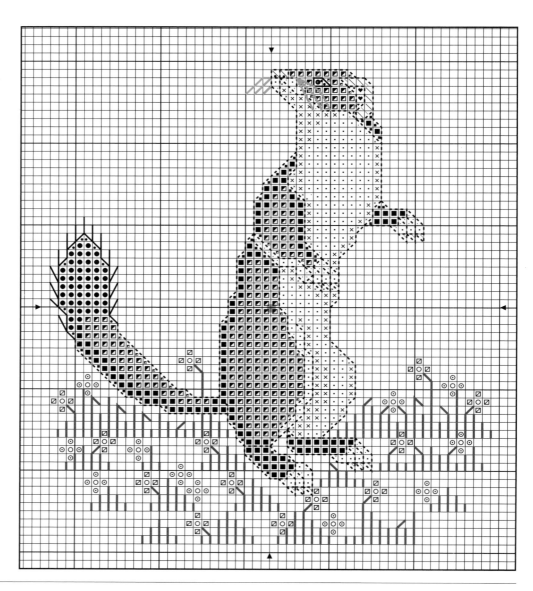

HOW TO STITCH

It is best to start stitching from the centre – this ensures an even amount of fabric all round the design. Find the centre of your fabric by folding it lightly in half both ways. The centre of the chart is indicated by a grey square.

Work the cross stitch first using two strands of stranded cotton.

When you have completed the cross stitch, you can work the following backstitch in one strand: dark brown for the stoat's outlines and details except for its tail; black to outline the stoat's tail; grey for its whiskers. Backstitch using two strands of green for the grass and flower stems.

Finally work the French knots in one strand: brown for the stoat's nostril; white for the eye highlight.

Once all the stitching is complete, trim the stitched design to 6x5in (15.2x12.7cm). Turn under two squares all round and stitch to the front of your rucksack with tiny invisible stitches.

YOU WILL NEED

- **14HPI aida** - 9x8in (22.9x20.3cm), cream
- **Stranded cotton** - as listed in the key
- **Tapestry needle** - size 24
- **Rucksack**
- **Usual sewing kit** - matching thread, needle, etc.

The stoat is distinguishable from the weasel by its black-tipped tail. It is one of the most ferocious of all mammalian predators and can look menacing to other animals when it stands erect on its hind legs to survey its surroundings.

STOAT KEY

ANCHOR	DMC	MADEIRA		COLOUR
Cross stitch in two strands				
001	White	White	· ·	White
050	605	0613	⊙⊙	Pink
145	334	0909	☑☑	Blue
290	973	0105	○○	Yellow
369	435	2010	◪◪	Light brown
370	433	2303	■■	Medium brown
398	415	1803	××	Grey
403	310	Black	●●	Black
914	3772	2310	♥♥	Dark flesh
4146	950	2309	◹◹	Light flesh
Backstitch all lines in one strand				
380	938	2005		Dark brown stoat outlines
398	415	1803		Grey whiskers
403	310	Black		Black eye, tail tip outlines & details
Backstitch all lines in two strands				
226	702	1306		Green grass & flower stems
Stitch French knots in one strand				
001	White	White	· ·	White eye highlight
380	938	2005	· ·	Dark brown nostrils

Our model was stitched using Anchor threads; the DMC and Madeira conversions are not necessarily exact colour equivalents.

Finished size: Stitch count 58 high x 52 wide
Fabric and approximate finished design area:
11HPI aida 5¼x4¾in
14HPI aida 4⅛x3⅝in   **18HPI** aida 3¼x2⅞in

Acknowledgements

The Publishers would like to thank the following people for their help in creating this book:

The Kit Company for framing and supplying kits

For supplying props for photography:

Leather Chairs of Bath (page 46)
Papyrus, Bath (page 46)
Tridias, Bath (page 42)
Villa Mimosa, Bath (page 46)
Waterstones, Bath (pages 22, 34, 42)

Thanks are also due to **Anchor Threads** for supplying fabric and threads

SUPPLIERS

For information on your nearest stockist of embroidery cotton, contact the following:

COATS AND ANCHOR

UK
Kilncraigs Mill
Alloa
Clackmannanshire
Scotland FK10 IEG

USA
Coats & Clark
P.O. Box 27067
Dept. CO1
Greenville
SC 29616

AUSTRALIA
Coats Patons Crafts
Thistle Street
Launceston
Tasmania
7250

DMC

UK
DMC Creative World Limited
62 Pullman Road
Wigston
Leicester LE8 2DY

USA
The DMC Corporation
Port Kearney Blc.
10 South Kearney
N.J. 07032-0650

AUSTRALIA
DMC Needlecraft Pty
P.O. Box 317
Earlswood 2206
NSW 2204

MADEIRA

UK
Madeira Threads (UK) Limited
Thirsk Industrial Park
York Road
Thirsk
North Yorkshire YO7 3BX

USA
Madeira Marketing Limited
600 East 9th Street
Michigan City
IN 46360

AUSTRALIA
Penguin Threads Pty Limited
25-27 Izett Street
Prahran
Victoria 3181

XXXXX